Real Estate

By J.Estate

Where Should You Put Your Money - Commercial Real Estate, Residential Properties Or Recreational Land

2nd Edition

Real Estate

Real Estate

Table of Contents

Introduction

It is no secret that real estate is a booming business. Everybody needs a house to stay in, a mall to shop at and a zoo for recreation. All these need to be based on properties and the first one pertains to residential properties, the second is an example of commercial property and the third one falls under recreational properties.

The demand for all three has gone up in the last decade, as more and more people have understood the value of buying, and renting out, these properties. Thousands of these go on sale on a weekly basis, with hundreds looking to buy and sell them in order to make a profit.

Real estate investments are a great option for any investor, no doubt, as it pays big to own a good property in an ideal location, however, it can get a bit tough when it comes to choosing the right type of property. You will have to do some research and understand what sort of deal will prove to be most lucrative. To help you make that choice, this book will provide you with all the information that you will need in regard to property investments.

In this book, we will look at all three of these properties viz. commercial, residential and recreational, in detail, and read on their individual pros and cons. There is also a bonus chapter on the important things that you must consider while looking for the ideal property.

I hope you find it easy to make your choice after you finish reading this book.

I thank you for choosing this book and hope you enjoy reading it.

Let us begin.

Chapter 1: Things To Consider While Investing In Real Estate

The intent of me writing this book is to share my knowledge of the real estate business with others who don't know how it actually works. In this first chapter of the book, we will look at the main things that you must consider when it comes to choosing the property. There is also an explanation of the things to bear in mind, when you proceed with the investments. Let us now read on each of these aspects.

Location

For any business, the location is of primary importance. Where the land is located, what facilities are close by, how accessible is the land, is electricity, water supply and telephone connection easily available? To understand if the property caters to all these questions, you must inspect all the details yourself. You must dedicate at least a week, or more, in visiting the site for yourself, to get a firsthand experience of what it feels like to own a property in that particular locality. You need to take note of the neighborhood and look at other properties that surround yours. Once you are satisfied with what you see, you can move to the next aspect.

Size

The next consideration should be the size of the property. Whether it is a house, or a piece of bare land, you must consider its size. You can ask for the details of the size and also measure it for yourself, just to be sure. You need to consider things such as; will it be an ideal size to rent out commercially? Whether it is ideal for a family of four? Is it in a good location for a mall to come up? Once you get an answer to all these questions, you can move to the next step.

Price

The next thing to consider is the price. You can choose the type of property depending on how much money is at your disposal. The best way to know if you are paying the correct price is by finding out the trending prices for properties in that locality. You can do so by performing a quick internet search or better still, ask people in the locality about it. They will know the rate per square foot, or per meter square, and you will be able to judge if you have been quoted the right price. If you think you are being over charged, then you can find out why and whether it can be negotiated.

Things included

Once you negotiate on the price, you must check for the things that will come along with the property. Generally, residential houses will come with a few fittings and fixtures and if the owner is keen on giving the house fully furnished, then everything present inside the house will be given away. Commercial properties come with underground storage units, display aisles; front desks etc. Recreational properties might include live stock, fences, equipment etc. You must make a note of everything that the owner is promising to give and check for them once you buy the property.

Boundary

Before you buy a property, you must check for its boundaries. This means that you must have a clear idea of where your property ends. Many owners will not specify it and you will be shocked to see another building barging into your land. This is especially important to consider for recreational properties and you need to get fencing done to know exactly where your property ends. This might also be important for commercial buildings and you must get high walls built to make for the boundary of your land.

Process

The purchase process comes next. For this, you will have to negotiate on the price and once the two of you agree upon a feasible value, you can initiate the payment process. Many people prefer to run the deal through their lawyer, just to make sure that everything is good. Once the lawyer approves of it, you can go ahead with the payment. After that is done, the seller will close the deal and you will become the absolute owner of the property. You will then have to look into the property tax details and other statutory paper work.

Finance

It is obvious that not everybody can afford to buy property using their own money. Some will need financing and this can be gained through commercial banks and money lenders. You must collect all your personal financial documents, documents in regard to the property and submit it to the institution. Once your loan is approved, you can pay the owner and start repaying your loan. But remember, banks will only give you 80% of the total amount and you will have to make arrangements for the remaining 20% of the price, of the property.

Future prospects

Remember to consider the future prospects of the property. For this, you must understand how the price of the property will rise and whether it will double in value in say 10 years' time. Similarly, you must find out if the area around your property will be developed, what might come next to your place, whether there will be other properties that will be dedicated to your type of business etc. Many people prefer to invest in places that are about to be developed, as they will get the property for a reasonable price, and once the area develops their property's value will rise.

Estate agent

It is always advisable to consult an estate agent. They will have access to the best properties on sale. When you wish to buy, you can simply brief them on what you are looking for and they will find the right property for you. They might charge you a fee for their service but it will be just a small percentage of the sale. They will also help you in availing finance, preparing the documents, title transfer etc. and you will have a smooth journey if you consult with thorough professionals.

Satisfaction

This is just a piece of advice. When you decide to invest in a property, make sure that you like the property. It should be to your liking in terms of the size, the price, the location etc. and don't blindly go with someone else's suggestions. You must spend time in going through every detail of the property and do several inspections to be satisfied with it. If you don't like a majority of the aspects in regard to the property then it is best that you not invest in it and look for another property that is to your taste and liking.

These form the different things to bear in mind while zeroing in on a property of your choice.

Chapter 2: Commercial Real Estate Properties

Now that we looked at the various aspects to bear in mind while choosing a property, we will now read on the meaning of commercial properties and look at what it means to invest in it.

What is it?

Commercial real estate properties pertain to those that are solely used for business purposes. So these will be used for hotels, shopping malls, offices, departmental stores etc.

Most of the property required for this type needs to be huge and must be capable of holding large numbers of people. The area should be well suited for the kind of business that is being operated on the property. Commercial properties are generally leased out, as collecting large amounts as rent can turn quite cumbersome.

Commercial property leases can be of 4 types and they are as follows.

- For a gross lease, the tenant is made to only pay the rent of the property and the owner takes care of the property tax, insurance and maintenance money
- For a single net lease, the tenant is made to pay the rent along with the property taxes
- For a double net, the tenant pays the rent for the property, the property tax and also the insurance
- The last type is the triple net, where the tenant pays the rents for the property, the property tax, insurance and also the maintenance

What is included?

Most commercial spaces come with standard things that are required to run any kind of business and these can include:

- A spacious parking space that is capable of fitting enough number of cars

- Lot of lights, both artificial and natural
- Good electric supply and ports
- Proper internet coverage
- Good potable water source
- Space for canteen or a lunch room
- Well built sanitation facilities
- Work stations/ cubicles

Some of these can be customized by the tenant after taking due permission from the owner. These are generally not separately charged and come free with the property, but if the owner has spent a lot of money in customizing the unit, then he might charge you extra for these facilities.

The pros

- One of the biggest advantages of owning a commercial space is that, you need not worry too much about its upkeep. Your tenants are most likely to be retailers and other businessmen, who will use your space to run their business; which means that they will have to open their doors to their clients and customers. And so, they will put in their best efforts to keep the office space clean and tidy.

- The next advantage is that, these people will be thorough professionals and you will have a good working relationship with them. There will not be many problems and any issues can be easily resolved.

- It is easier for you to arrive at a leasing policy and all you have to do is collect from the previous owner their pricing policy and based on it, remodel yours. You will have a fair idea of how much needs to be charged and you will not have to run around looking for a pricing policy to help you out.

- When you rent out for commercial purposes, you will be able to make a lot of money within a short period of time. If you lease it out, then you can choose to do it for a long period of time and in the mean time, use the money to invest and grow its value. You will have a good chance at repaying all of your loans by leasing out your commercial property. It will be best if you choose the triple net lease system, as that will work to your advantage.

- Most commercial businesses will run during the morning hours and so, you do not have to deal with random problems in the middle of the night. Once the office hours are over, you can go to bed peacefully.

The cons

- The most important disadvantage to consider while choosing a commercial property to invest in is the high rate of initial capital that will be required for it. You will need a lot of money, probably ranging in the millions, to start a commercial property investment. Add to it the price of repair and up keep and you will probably be looking at a few thousands more and that king of money is tough to arrange for.

- One big disadvantage of owning a big commercial property is that, you might have to rent it out to 2 or more tenants. This means that you will have to deal with several types of people, and they might not all get along with each other. Trying to manage such people might turn into nightmare. You will have to try and get them to like each other, which might be no less than a herculean task.

- Commercial properties are open to the public, which means that they are likely to get damaged more. There can be hundreds of footfalls a day and several cars will access the parking area. Some people might end up damaging the property and rash driving might cause issues in the parking area. All this can turn into a big maintenance headache for the owner and you might have to avail the help of a third party to take care of the maintenance and up keep of the building.

- When it comes to the overall appearance of the building, you might have to take the opinion of all your tenants and decide on a look that satisfies everybody. This can take up a lot of time and you might not have a chance to lease it out as soon as you buy it. If your current tenant is leaving and another one is coming in, then they might have other requests and catering to these might further cost you.

These form the various advantages and disadvantages of owning commercial real estate properties and you can go through them again to make up your mind.

Chapter 3: Residential Real Estate Properties

In the previous chapter, we looked at the advantages and disadvantages of investing in commercial properties and now, we will shift focus to residential properties. The second preferred type of properties to invest in is residential properties and let us read on them in detail.

What is it?

Residential properties are those that are used for residential purposes. So independent houses, villas, condominiums, apartments, hostels etc. are all residential properties. These are places where people live, and they are not allowed to carry out any business unless the owner approves of it.

Most owners specify the number of people that can live in the house. This is important as the more the people, the more the maintenance required. If it is meant for a family of 4, then the owner will specify it before renting it out. If at any time he finds that more number of people are living in the house then he will summon them.

Single family properties refer to individual houses that can be rented out to a single family and multifamily properties are several houses where many families can be allowed one house each. All these houses are generally present in the same building or complex. These can be two flat, three flat, four flat or an apartment building.

Residential properties can be charged on the following basis:

- Rent only, where the tenant pays the rent alone and the owner pays the maintenance
- Rent plus maintenance where the tenant pays both these charges
- Lease refers to collecting a lump sum amount at the beginning and renting out the property for a few years

Real Estate

What is included?
When it comes to residential properties the standard fittings and fixtures are provided and they are as follows:

- Ceiling fans
- Tube lights
- Switch ports
- Toilets
- Tiles
- Cupboards
- Parking space
- Furniture (optional)
- Chimney(optional)

Including these things will help you command a better price for you property. You can make the house look as good as possible so that people are drawn to your place.

The pros
- The main advantage of investing in residential properties is that, you will not require a large sum of money to begin with. You can manage to buy a residential property within a few thousand dollars and do not have to invest millions, unless you are looking for a palatial property.

- Availing finance for your property is simple. You will only have to submit a few papers and your loan can be approved within a couple of weeks. You can avail up to 80% of the price. You can buy and rent out your property in a matter of a single month.

- You can make use of your loan and mortgage money to avail tax deductions. You stand a chance to save a lot of money, which you can use to do up the house, and house renovation is also tax deductible.

- The cost per square foot will be much lesser than commercial properties. You will get a larger piece of land and a bigger building if you choose to invest in residential properties.

- If you own a building that has many houses then you can choose to live in one of them. This will help you keep an eye on the house and the tenants. You will also be able to maintain the building and not worry about any damages being caused.

The cons

- One disadvantage of owning a single residential property is that, you must have tenants in constant supply. If you lose one tenant then it means losing all your rent. So it is slightly risky to invest in single family properties and you must try and have at least two or more residential properties to have a rolling and consistent rent coming your way.

- The maintenance of residential buildings can be headache as most tenants will not take care of the house. If there is a leak or a pipe break in the middle of the night then you will have to rush to get it fixed. The cost for repairs will also be quite high and you will probably have to have a separate budget for repairs.

- If you wish to give away your residential property for commercial use then you will have to take due permission from a lot of authorities. You might get into trouble if you don't take these permissions and for this reason, it is important that you take due permission for a commercial business to be conducted in your house or apartment.

- If you are renting out a hostel, then you can forget about living in peace. Hostels are mostly occupied by youngsters who will not care about the upkeep of the house. They will also constantly rotate, and you will probably have to receive rent from a different person every month. There is also the danger of several people living in the building at one time and violating your rule of allowing only a certain number to occupy the houses.

- Some tenants might indulge in sub letting without your knowledge. This will cause them to profit from your property and they will pay you lesser than what they are making from it. This will cause you to undergo losses and so, it becomes important to keep an eye on your tenant once you rent out your property.

These form the various pros and cons of residential properties and you can read these once more to arrive at your decision.

Real Estate

Chapter 4: Recreation Real Estate Properties

In the last two chapters, we looked at commercial properties and residential properties and now, we will look at the third type known as recreational properties.

In this chapter I will give you information on the meaning and pros and cons of investing in recreational properties.

What is it?

As the name suggests, recreational properties are used for recreational purposes. They are meant to be used for the purpose of finding pleasure and joy.

Most recreational properties pertain to farms, ranches, water fronts, land for zoo, land for wild life reserves etc. As you can see, nature plays an important role in making a piece of land recreation worthy.

You can buy a house in front of a sea or a cabin in the middle of the woods and it can be made into your recreational property. If you wish to open it to the pubic then you can consider turning a piece of land into a wilderness reserve or a zoo.

It is possible for you to rent out these properties or lease the plot of land. But for this, your land needs to "zoned" first. Zoning refers to the control that the authorities exercise over a piece of land and decide on how the particular piece can be used. So, if you wish to use it for personal use all through the year then you will have to take permission for it. Similarly, if you wish to start a reserve or rent it out then you need to get due permission from the authorities. Remember that most recreational lands are seasonally zoned by the local municipal authorities. It is possible to change the zoning but will take considerable time and effort.

What is included?

Most recreational lands come with the following

- Fences and gates
- Trees, plants, shrubs
- Sheds
- Cabins
- Water bodies
- Livestock, wild animals (rare)
- Animal feeders
- Animal waste disposal systems

These are all the standard things that will come with your recreational land and you will have to inspect each of these thoroughly before you make your choice.

The pros

- Being close to nature and enjoying a fresh environment is the biggest advantage of owning recreational land. This is the exact reason why more and more people are interested in using these as their retirement homes. It is also ideal for young children as they will have a chance to live in a natural environment that is free from dust, dirt and other pollutants. They will benefit from overall well being and their mental, emotional and physical needs will be met with, naturally.

- Renting out a cabin overlooking the mountains or in front of a large sea is sure to bring in huge amounts of money. There can be a lot of adventure promoting amenities such as hiking, rafting, fishing, cycling etc. and this will draw in hordes of nature loving crowds. You can rent it out to a hotel or a lodge or just as vacation rentals. You will have the chance to turn your recreational property into a major money maker.

- The presence of animals and wild life in general, will be a hit with those interested in fishing, hunting and watching. Being in the presence of animals will make you feel blessed and give you an opportunity to get close to nature. You will also do your bit in conserving the wild life and take care of the area for them to lead a normal life.

- It is believed that the sense of community in recreational lands runs quite deep. Everybody loves the company of others and people get to live in a close knit community. Children will get a chance to go to schools where only a few other pupils will be present and this will help them avail individual attention.

- If you choose a property that is aloof, then you can avail it for a cheap price. If the area gets developed in the future then you will stand a chance to make a huge profit out of your property.

The cons
- One of the biggest cons of recreational property is getting adjusted to a remote life. Most people are born and brought up in the city and transitioning to a life in the wilderness will prove to be quite difficult.

- Maintaining the facility can be extremely difficult as many things will have to be taken care of. You will have to do all the cleaning, chop the wood, trim the bushes, feed the animals, take care of their waste, maintain the cabin, shovel the snow, get rid of dead leaves etc. All of this will turn out to be mundane activities and will be quite labor intensive.

- Some farfetched areas will not have proper drainage systems, water facilities, heating systems, availability of cooking gas etc. These areas will also not have any sort of network coverage and internet and telephone cables will not be available to avail connections.

- Recreational lands are susceptible to extreme weather conditions. You will have to be ready to accept anything that nature throws at you. Right from a hurricane to heavy snow to heat waves, you will be exposed to extremes and must be strong enough to live through these.

Real Estate

- Wild animals are amazing no doubt but can be dangerous and might attack you or your family members. It will be doom if a tiger family makes its way to your cabin. Smaller animals such as rats and raccoons will invade your house on a regular basis and it will be very difficult for you to control them.

- Expansion will be a problem as you will have to seek appropriate permission to expand your land. You cannot decide today and start expanding your land or cabin tomorrow. You will have to await approval from the authorities and only then can you begin work.

- Employment is a big problem on recreational lands. The most you can do is clean other people's farms, chop their wood, teach at a community school, become a tour guide etc. But these might be seasonal jobs and might not last all year long.

Chapter 5: Tips on How to Buy Real Estate

There are a lot of things that one has to consider before buying real estate. After all, your real estate is going to be what takes your business to the next level. It is the commodity that you are going to be selling later on in order to earn your living!

Hence, this chapter includes a list of tips that you should apply while scouting real estate to buy. Make sure that you consider each and every tip before buying property in order to ensure that the property you do buy is worth selling in the long run.

Clear Debts and Avoid Amassing New Debts Before You Buy a New House

One of the biggest reasons that you are unable to buy good property is that you do not have a good credit rating. Your credit rating is a way for people who are looking to sell their houses to ascertain whether you are a trustworthy person to sell to or not.

After all, it is highly unlikely that you are going to have assets that are liquid enough to facilitate you buying a house outright. You are going to have to use credit in order to purchase the house, and in order to do so it is very important that you do not move your money around too much.

What this means is that you should avoid any big purchases starting from six months before you plan to buy a house. Buying things using your credit card racks up debt which lowers your credit score. If you pay your debts off quickly your credit score is raised, but until then it remains too low.

This would make you seem untrustworthy. Having a large amount of debt prior to approaching a home that you intend to buy would result in most home owners considering you untrustworthy. The general notion is that you have a lot of debt that you have to pay off you might become unreliable while paying off the home that you are currently purchasing.

It is also highly recommended that you do not get any new credit cards before you approach a seller in order to purchase a new home. A new credit card means a lower overall credit rating because you have not had the chance to pay off any debts on your new credit, so you should avoid it if you can.

Get Pre-Approved For a Mortgage

First things first, you need to understand that qualifying for a mortgage is vastly different from getting approved for a mortgage. This is because the stamps of approval or qualification have very different connotations and thus say different things about your financial reliability.

It is very easy to get pre qualified for a loan. So easy, in fact, that telling a potential seller that you are pre qualified won't really do much boost his or her opinion of you in any significant or meaningful way. Getting pre approved for a mortgage, on the other hand, is a completely different matter.

This is because the process of getting pre approved is much more difficult and time consuming, and not everybody ends up getting approved for a mortgage or a loan. If you are qualified and you head to the bank to get a loan, that is when the approval process starts.

Essentially getting approved is impossible unless you have an excellent credit rating. This is because in order to get approved for a mortgage you need to prove that you are going to be able to pay the mortgage back without missing payments regularly.

When a bank pre approves you for a mortgage, it has essentially already granted you the mortgage. The executives at the bank will have looked into your financial history and will have ascertained to a large degree how financially reliable you are.

It is for these reasons that a seller will be more willing to sell to you if you are pre approved for a mortgage. Hence, you can save yourself a lot of time and effort be planning your buy in advance and getting yourself pre approved for a mortgage before you approach any prospective sellers.

Real Estate

Mind Your Property Lines

The survey is one of the most important parts of the pre buying process. It points out any areas of concern, and ensures that you head into this purchase with your eyes open, fully aware of anything that might cause you problems in the future.

One of the most important areas you should focus on during the survey is the property lines. Having indistinct, undefined or irregular property lines can result in two problems that can become very troublesome if they are not resolved before the house has been purchased and the deeds have been transferred to your name.

The first of these two problems is obviously disputes with your neighbor. If your property lines overlap with those of another neighbor, there can be a legal dispute. Additionally, having property lines that encroach on an area that should technically belong to your neighbors is an ethical offense, and can very quickly turn into a legal one if your neighbors get annoyed by it.

In order to avoid long and unnecessary complications with your home, it is a good idea to monitor the property lines before your property has been bought. The legal problems your neighbors can bring in are worth fixing before the property is yours.

Another problem that property lines can cause involves property tax. If you have property lines that extend to an irregular shape and you are unaware of this, you might end up paying more property tax than you are aware of. This is because property tax is calculated on the basis of square footage.

Hence, it is important to know just what your property lines are so that you can get an exact estimate of how much property tax you are going to pay, instead of having to get an unpleasant surprise on tax day.

Don't Wait for the Right Time

There is no way to predict the real estate market, and that's just the way it always has been and will be unless a major change in the way the real estate market works develops.

Real Estate

The real estate market is a great market to trade in and earn a living, but one major problem with it is that it simply cannot be predicted to do anything. This means that you absolutely cannot wait for the right time in order to purchase a property you want.

This is one of the major problems that people find with the real estate market. Trying to time the market can only result in you missing out on opportunities that would have earned you enormous amounts of money, because the real estate industry functions in a different way.

In order to make it big in real estate you need to be assertive and confident and you need to know how to market things. You need to know how to turn a dilapidated old house into a mansion, and to sell it in a way that people have no idea how it used to be before you renovated.

Hence, the best thing to do if you want to make good money in real estate is to look hard, find a house that you love or you think you can fix up well and buy it. If you like a house this means that the house has several likable qualities. This means that a lot of people will agree with you and see the same lovely qualities in this home.

Real estate is cyclical in a way that no one can predict. When it goes up and when it goes down is completely random, so don't miss out on your dream purchase because of the way it is acting.

Don't Judge a House by Its Size

This is a common rule in the real estate business. If you want to make it big in real estate, you never buy the biggest house on the block.

This might seem odd to you. After all, everybody wants the biggest house on the block! Everyone wants to live in that mansion and lord over the rest. The house that is the most expensive can be sold for the most as well, right?

Your logic is sound, but it doesn't take into account one fact. Everybody wants the biggest house, but very few people ever end up buying it. This means that if you buy this enormous house you are going to severely limit your potential buyers, due to the simple fact that not many people are going to be able to afford to buy the house no matter how much they want it.

This also means that your house is never going to appreciate much. Since the price is already so high, there is a very limited amount of growth space that you get for the price no matter how much you do to it. This contrasts with houses in the same neighborhood which are worth less.

It would be a smarter move to buy a smaller, maybe even the smallest and most dilapidated house in said neighborhood if it has a big house in it. This is fixing the house up and making it competitive will not cost nearly as much as buying the bigger house, but the returns you are going to get from selling this smaller house are going to be much more significant.

Hence, unless you are planning to live in it yourself, never buy the biggest house in the neighborhood.

Don't Treat Mortgage like Rent

Paying off a mortgage does in a lot of ways seem like rent. After all, you are paying a monthly payment that is similar in amount to rent, and in some cases, such as if you are paying off your mortgage over a very long period of time, can be a lot lower than rent.

So what makes mortgage so different from rent? Why don't people just save up for a down payment and buy houses all of the time? In order to understand this difference you are going to have had to own a home some time in your past.

The major difference between renting a home and owning one is that there are several costs that are not included in your monthly payment. These include your maintenance costs, since you are the landlord there is nobody but you who is going to fix up your home when something breaks, and your monthly, bimonthly or biannual payment to the homeowners association.

A lot of rentals also do not come with utility bills, a fixed amount for which is most often included in the rent itself. However, if you own the house you are going to have to pay the bills. Additionally, you are going to have to pay a significant amount of property tax if you own a home, something that you would not have to do if you were simply renting it.

Hence, it is very important that you keep these additional expenses in mind when you are buying a house. Don't just think that you are going to have to make monthly payments and nothing beyond them. Doing this is shortsighted, and will result in a lot of financial problems that are going to decrease the value of your property.

Go for Your Instincts, Not Emotions

A lot of people end up buying a house because they fall in love with it. It might remind them of their childhood homes, it might have a pool which they have always wanted, or it might have some other kind of feature which ends up making feel as though they have to buy the house.

This is perfectly fine if you intend to live in the house, even though it is highly not recommended. However, if you are planning on selling a house, buying based on your emotions is one of the worst things that you could possibly do. Remember, you are not planning to marry the house that you are buying; you are planning to sell it.

The main driving factor behind your purchase of a house should be instinct. Instinct is what will make you look at a house, even one that is completely broken down, and see it for what it will actually be worth in the future. It is what makes you see the neighborhood around the house for being clean, safe and a place where people would really want to live, which makes the buy worth it in the long run.

In essence, instinct makes you see the bigger pictures, to look at a house and see its commercial value. Emotions makes you want to buy it for the color or the floor tiles, it has absolutely nothing to do with how much money you can make off of the house after you have fixed it up and let it appreciate for a few years.

Be smart about the house you are buying. If you want real estate to be your job, you are going to use your instinct when hunting for places.

Use a Home Inspector

You might be considering a home inspector for your home, but are having second thoughts because it costs around a couple hundred dollars. What you don't realize is that these couple hundred dollars might just end up saving you thousands of dollars in the wrong run.

Real estate is about making good purchases and avoiding bad ones. You know what sells and what doesn't, but you aren't an expert on homes, which means that there are a lot of things that might be wrong with a place that you will have missed which could end up devaluing your house if you are not careful.

A home inspector's job is to perform a thorough inspection of a house and to find any faults with it. If he or she does not find any faults, you can rest assured that a professional has deemed your house free of any problems in the future.

However, if an inspector finds faults in the home you are thinking of purchasing, you can use the faults that have been found to leverage a lowered buying price from the seller.

This is very important, because if you tell the seller about the problems yourself the seller could discredit your findings saying that you are not qualified. However, if a professional home inspector relays these problems for you, you will have a real reason to buy the house for a much lower price than you would otherwise.

Additionally, getting a professional inspection done is a way to ensure that the house you are buying is being bought on instinct or emotion. If you see something in the house, chances are that the inspector is going to see it too. There really is no better way to get an objective opinion on the home you are intending to buy.

Be Careful With Your Opening Bid

The opening bid is one of the most important parts of buying real estate. There is actually a lot of misconception around the opening bid. First and foremost, a lot of people tend to think that the lower the price they offer in the opening bid, the better the offer they are going to get in the long run.

This is not true however. Offering too little with the opening bid might end up offending the seller, which means that he or she would not be willing to sell you the property later on.

If you are looking to make a competitive opening bid, there are two main factors that you need to keep in mind. First and foremost is what you can afford. You are the one who is going to be paying for the house, so why offer something that you simply can't pay? This is also important because it will prevent you from overbidding.

The second thing that you should keep in mind while bidding for your potential house is its worth in your eyes. Obviously, the two numbers are not going to be far apart if you have done your homework by keeping your credit score up and getting yourself preapproved for a mortgage. Hence, unless you are shopping for a home in an area that is outside a reasonable budget, you should be able to find a happy medium and haggle your way from there.

You should also look into whether the property taxes for the home have been paid or not. A lot of homeowners have unpaid property tax, which means that you can use this information to leverage a lower price, especially considering that the homeowner failed to tell you in the first place.

Research the Neighborhood

When someone buys a house, they don't just do it for the house itself. Another very important factor that affects people who are thinking of buying a home is the neighborhood the home is in. People want a safe environment for their children; they want a place that is respectable and accepting.

Hence, it is very important that you stake out the neighborhood just in case before you actually buy a home. A lot of neighborhoods look good in the middle of the afternoon, but once the sun sets the shape and face of the block completely changes.

Real Estate

Nobody wants to live in an unsavory area, so you need to do your homework. Otherwise you might end up buying a great home in a bad neighborhood, and no one is going to want to buy there. As a result you are going to end up spending money on a great place that no one will want to buy because they don't think that the neighborhood is worth the quality of the house, no matter how high the quality of the house itself is.

The first thing you can do is to sweep the neighborhood once after you have seen the house. Check to see how far the nearest shops are and pay close attention to the schools. About a fifth of your house's value depends on the quality of the schools nearby, so you can use bad schools as a leverage to lower the price or as a reason not to buy at all.

In order to really be sure of the neighborhood you should come back and see what's going on at random times during the day. A good idea will be to drive through the neighborhood on your way to your office every day.

Chapter 6 Tips on How to Sell Real Estate

Buying real estate is one thing, selling it is another. The difference between both of these areas of real estate is so vast that it warranted a completely different chapter. In fact, this chapter is even longer than the previous one because it involves so much more information.

Selling your house is a big deal, because it is where you are going to earn money from and improve your reputation within the real estate industry. Hence, what follows is a list of tips to help you sell your home faster and with ease.

Mind the Smell of Your Home

You may be thinking that smell is unimportant. After all, your potential buyers, all of the people that come to look at your house for a viewing are going to realize that the house is uninhabited and that the smell will be gone once people move in right?

This is actually completely wrong. When people come into a house, smell is the first thing that they notice and it affects their opinion of the house. A commonly unknown fact is that smell is one thing that we associate most to memory. Hence, if they smell something funny while they are viewing your home, they are going to associate this smell with your home and probably won't end up buying it.

One of the biggest ways in which you can spoil the smell of your home is by using mothballs. Mothballs smell awful no matter how useful they are. This doesn't mean that you should not use them because they do fulfill a useful function without which your house will probably never get sold.

What you should do is mask the smell of the mothballs as much as you can. Use air freshener just before your potential buyers come into the room, but for a long term solution it would be a good idea to light scented candles or to place potpourri in each room of your home.

Another great idea is to bake something that smells good and offer it to the people who are coming to view your home. Not only will this leave a great impression on them, it's also going to fill the house with the sweet smell of the baked goods. This homely smell is what people are going to associate to the memory of viewing your property!

Lighting Matters Too

Smell is not the only thing that can put people off your home. Have you ever been in a room with dim lighting? If the room is well furnished and the dim light comes from several elegant lamps that throw off soft light and are meant to provide dim light, it can look very classy and comfortable.

However, if the light is dim because it comes from an insufficient source, such as drawn curtains or blinds or a single light bulb, and is in a room that is empty of furniture, which your property is going to be when people come to see it, it just ends up making the room look dreary and depressing.

Hence, if you don't want people to get put off your property because it was dreary and depressing, it is very important that you mind the way that the house they are viewing is lit.

The most important way that you can do this is to flood your home with as much natural light as possible. Doing this will ensure that your house looks good and clean, as natural light is always more attractive than artificial light and tends to cook away bacteria that cause bad smells as well.

You should also use lamps in every room in order to make the house look as inviting as possible and to make it so that your guests are able to see clearly while they are in your property. The key is to help your potential buyers associate a good sense of homeliness to your property.

By doing these things you are going to help your potential buyers picture the home that your property could become for them. Depressing and dreary lighting will get in the way of that picture and put them off your property.

Decorate Your Home

One big problem with your house if you were reading the previous tip and it applied to you is that you have not furnished it. Lighting is incredibly important but at the day it can only do so much to hide the absence of furniture.

Remember, the previous tip was all about making your property look like a home to you potential buyers instead of just an empty house with no character, a place that is cold and devoid of human warmth. An even better way to do this is to decorate your home.

You can set up your house in a way that would make it seem attractive and modern. Buyers really like looking at modern homes that have that sleek, shiny look and decorating your house in such a way might provide buyers with an impetus to buy your property as quickly as possible.

One problem with decorating your property is that it tends to get expensive. It might help you sell your house for a higher price but doing it in the first place requires money that you might not have to spare, especially if you are paying off the mortgage for a home.

In such situations you can scale down the furnishing to only provide the basics, a skeleton of what could be in a way. If you really can't afford to spend any money, just updating the wall paper or getting the house walls painted could really boost the way it looks to potential buyers.

Doing such things is an important part of selling your property for a good price, because at the end of the day perception is everything. If people perceive that your property is a good buy they will buy it, and what decoration will especially help you with is hiding the flaws in your home.

Make a Good First Impression

If you have furnished your home incredibly and made it spick and span, kept it clean, removed all bad smells and lit it up like a Christmas tree you have done well, but you might be forgetting one of the most important parts.

No matter what you do, the front lawn, front door or whatever entry passageway your home possesses is going to give your potential buyers their first impression of the property that you are trying to sell them.

You would be surprised at how much of an effect the front door actually has on a potential customer. Even if your potential buyers love everything about your house, if the first impression wasn't as good as it should have been they might end up having second thoughts and reconsidering at the last moment.

On the other hand, if your property has a great entrance, with a moved lawn and a lovely entrance door, your potential buyers might end up ignoring the rest of the flaws that your property might have (none of which it should have if you have done adequate prep work) simply because they got a good first impression of the place.

This is an inexplicable but very important role that psychology plays in the selling of your home. By painting your door, an act so simple that it might even feel inconsequential to you and you might end up ignoring it completely thinking that it's not important, you might be making the difference between a buy and a pass.

Pay close attention the first impression your potential buyers get of your home. You might not know it, but that is because you look at homes as commodities to sell, and they look at them as places to live.

Make Sure Nobody You Know Visits

This is one rule that applies in a big way if you were living in the home that you are selling now, but it also applies if your friends know that you are selling your property.

Remember, your property is being viewed for sale; it is not an opportunity for you to catch up with friends. You should let everyone know that they should not interrupt the experience that your potential buyers are having by coming over for a visit because it might break the illusion that the buyers are having.

It's all about helping the buyers imagine what their lives would be like if they were living in this house. They simply would not be able to do that if the people that the owner of the home is friends with come by for a visit while they are looking at the property.

This means that you need to get your family and relatives out of your property as well. Take them away for a fun day out and let your realtor handle everything, because seeing your own relatives living in the home will prevent potential buyers from looking at the house and seeing themselves living in it.

Your realtor is a reliable resource, so ask him or her how you can ensure an ambience that would help people to think of themselves living in your home.

Get Rid of Personal Items

Before a viewing, it is extremely important that you get rid of anything in your house that can be defined as yours, as in anything that can indicate that someone is living in the house. This means all pictures and certificates with your name on it, all awards and trophies in your kids rooms, essentially everything that would prevent people from feeling like they could live in this property should be put away until the viewing is over.

Hire a Realtor

This is a very important tip, and one that you should definitely apply if you are thinking of finally selling off your property.

A realtor is a professional that deals with the sale of homes and can handle things that you simply would not be able to. This is very similar to why you would be hiring a home inspector before you buy your home, the reasoning behind which is quite similar to the reasoning behind hiring a realtor.

Your job is to find homes that might be valuable in the long run, buy them, fix them up and sell them at the highest price you can manage. However, sales are a completely different matter, and certainly not one that you should handle yourself unless you know yourself to be skilled in this particular area.

By hiring a realtor you are also going to have a friendly face that is not invested in your own financial future to sell the home, which means that they will not become passionate while dealing with customers. You might not be able to be so impartial if you try to handle potential buyers during the viewing yourself.

A realtor knows what to do when something goes wrong, and will not panic. Instead, he or she will probably handle the situation a lot better than you will. A realtor will also be able to get your house as high a price as possible. After all, he or she will be getting a commission, so that higher the price that the house sells at the more money that will be going into their own pocket, so you can rest assured that they will work hard!

Get Out of the House

If there is a viewing and your family does not live there, that's no reason for you to stick around. You have absolutely no reason to be there during the viewing, especially if you have a realtor who is handling everything for you.

In fact, you being there is probably going to result in problems for a lot of people who would be objectively viewing the house and considering whether they are going to live there or not, especially since you have a vested interest in selling the place.

If you are there during the viewing, you might end up pressuring people to buy your house. If someone asks a question that is valid, you might end up getting passionate while defending your house. This is, of course, natural considering you have spent so much time and effort getting this house ready for a viewing, and that these people are looking at it with a critical eye.

What you will fail to understand is that this critical eye is very necessary for them. It was the same critical eye that you had while you were attempting to purchase a home, even though your intention was not to live in it but to sell it. Just imagine what these people will feel, especially considering that they intend to live in this property!

You being there could also cause a clash of management. Your realtor is supposed to be managing the viewings and probably would have a strategy about tackling problems and making sure that people have a good experience while they are viewing the home in order to make them interested in buying it. If you are there you might make his or her job more difficult than it should be which could bring the whole thing crashing down!

Focus on Your Kitchen and Bathroom

Decoration is extremely important, as has already been mentioned in a section prior to this one. What has also been mentioned in a section prior to this one is that decoration can be too expensive for you at this point considering you have so much money invested in the house already.

The most important parts of your home are the kitchen and bathroom, so if you invest in keeping these areas looking as attractive, stylish and overall appealing as possible you have done the vast majority of the work decoration will have done anyway.

The first things you need to do in order to make your kitchen and bathroom attractive is to obviously clean it out. Nothing puts people off more than a dirty bathroom, no matter how great the rest of the house is. Make your house shine so that the people viewing it can see what a great bathroom you have.

You will also be spending money to renovate the house. Make the bathroom and kitchen your priorities. Nobody really wants much in a bedroom. After all, bedrooms are what you customize on your own with pictures and posters and whatnot. However, a kitchen is something that everybody wants to be as top of the line as possible.

It is highly recommended that you add a built in fridge to your kitchen, and to ensure that the oven that you provide is top of the line, even if you don't intend on including it in the sale price, as it will give your buyers a great impression.

You should also make your bathroom sleek and modern with the new commodes that seem built into the wall rather than the floor as they contribute to a modern look in your home.

Talk to Your Realtor

You and your realtor have a very important professional relationship, so it is very important that the two of you keep a line of communication open between you at all times, especially since you intend to not be at home while the viewing is going on.

Ask your realtor as many questions and raise as many concerns as you want before you begin showing your house to potential buyers. You can even ask him or her what you should do to your bathroom and kitchen, because realtors will know what potential buyers would want to see in a home that they are thinking of buying.

Once the viewing has begun, it is recommended that you go to a coffee shop, sit and do something that ideally does not command too much of your attention because you might be needed at any time.

The realtor could, for example, need to contact you if a potential buyer has haggled a little and offered a slightly reduced price for your home. If you are unavailable you might end up losing the buyer, because the realtor would be unable to agree to a reduced price if you do not sign off on it.

Additionally, your realtor might need you to answer a few questions for her or him about the home if he or she does not already know the answer to these questions. These questions might involve the history of the home, past owners, past neighbors, the state of the neighborhood and so on.

The bottom line is, if you communicate with your realtor the experience is going to be much easier and stress free than if you are not. Keep your phone on, ask as many questions as possible, and apart from these things try not to get in their way!

Professional Cleaners and Fumigators need to be hired

Real Estate

Obviously if you want your home to be attractive to potential buyers you need to clean it up before you have people over to see it and potentially buy it. However, a major oversight is to avoid cleaning the house in places that don't normally get cleaned.

You will definitely need to hire a professional cleaning service. You might be inspired to clean your house yourself but it is an enormous project to undertake and you probably will not end up cleaning as thoroughly as a team of experienced cleaners would.

Much like with realtors and home inspectors, this just something that you will have to do. It is an investment in the future of your home and will help you to attract more buyers and prevent interested people from getting discouraged by dirt.

Additionally, it is highly recommended that you hire a fumigator just in case. You might not have seen any bugs in your property, but viewers who are dead set on finding something wrong just so they can drag the price down might, especially if your property has been empty for a long period of time.

A fumigator will ensure that your property is completely clean of bugs, and is just another investment that you must make in order to make your home as presentable as possible to potential buyers.

An added benefit of hiring a fumigator is that you will not have to use mothballs. If you remember the very first tip in this list, you will remember that the smell of your home is one of the most important things that could factor into the way your house is perceived by potential buyers. A fumigator will allow you to rest assured that no bugs will be in your home without your use of mothballs.

Flowers at the Front Entrance

Once again, first impressions tend to be one of the most important deciding factors that will come into play when people consider buying your house.

Putting flowers up at the front entrance handles a lot of problems that you might face while setting your home up for a viewing. Firstly it would help you give a good first impression, a fact which has already been stated. When people come in and see bright flowers on a table, the emotions they feel are going to affect everything else that they see in your house.

Additionally, the flowers are probably going to smell good. In fact, it is highly recommended that you get flowers that are fragrant. This will help you to fill your home with a good smell that is completely natural and free of all chemicals, something that air fresheners simply cannot do. Flowers are also a lot better than potpourri, which tends to smell artificial and far too strong as well.

One final thing that flowers are going to really help you with is the appearance of the interior of your home. Placing something like flowers at your front entrance is a great idea because it helps the first impressions as well as the interior design. Flowers spread their colors to everything around them, so they can help spruce up empty houses and help your lights to really get the dreariness out of your property.

Do yourself a favor and follow this tip. It costs barely anything and provides not one but three whole benefits to three different problems that you could face while showing your home to viewers. Surprisingly, no other single item is as useful as flowers!

Don't Be Desperate for a Buy

If you absolutely must be at your property while a viewing is going on, I must say I can't blame you. After all, your property is the result of a long, long effort on your part to get going in the real estate business, so you would naturally want to be around in order to make sure that absolutely nothing goes wrong.

However, there is a certain rule that you will need to follow no matter what it is that you want. This rule might make the difference between a buy and a pass.

Do not show desperation. If customers ask you objective questions, answer them to the best of your ability, but don't let it show that you need to sell the house. This is especially important when potential buyers make that all important first bid. If you fumble about and let them know just how much you need to sell the house it is going to give them a real basis for negotiation.

Knowing that you're desperate will allow them to bid low and stay firm with their bid no matter what you say. After all, your home is your livelihood, and selling it for any amount is going to earn you money. The key is to earn as much money with your property as possible.

This becomes very important if your property has sat on the market for a while. Your property might not get sold for a long time simply because the market is down. This is no reason to be desperate however, at least in front of potential buyers.

You need to keep your poker face on so that they think that you have enough buyers wanting this house that you can confidently ask for a lot of money.

Put Towels in the Bathroom

You might feel that doing so is unnecessary, but by this logic renovating your bathroom becomes unnecessary as well. The whole point of this process is to make it easier for potential buyers to imagine themselves living in this home.

Having towels in the bathroom will give them the impression that the house is livable. It is a big part of making the house as cozy and comfortable as possible so that potential buyers come and see that there is a lot of potential to be had in a home with so many great features.

You can also put rugs down in the bathroom as well, along with a shower curtain. Again, these things will help to make your bathroom look as livable as possible, giving your property a homely feel.

Put Appliances in Your Kitchen

This is a little trick that a lot of real estate businessmen use. If you add appliances to your kitchen, you are not just going to give your kitchen a much more homely feel, you are also going to give your potential buyers the illusion that the kitchen is actually much nicer that it really is.

When potential buyers and viewers enter a kitchen, they tend not to notice that the appliances are there. They just take in the overall ambience of the kitchen. This can help you to give your kitchen a look that will reel your buyers in.

You don't have to sell the appliances with the house. Just place them in the kitchen the day of the viewing in order to give your viewers a more homely experience when they enter. If a buyer asks if the appliances in your kitchen are going to be sold with the house, tell that that they are not and then offer to sell them for extra!

Do Not Get Emotional

No matter how much work and effort has gone into buying this house and making it adequate for selling on the open market, you need to realize that you are a professional now, and need to comport yourself in such a way.

This means that you absolutely cannot let your emotions get in the way of how you interact with your viewers when you make your house open to such an event. You need to act on instinct and give your viewers objective answers to their questions!

This is because emotions and passions tend to obstruct sales technique. If you are at the place where your business is being conducted and are handling it yourself, you need to keep this in mind.

Prepare for the Long Haul

Sometimes properties are available for sale for months at a time. This is just the way that the real estate industry works. If this happens, you absolutely should not let yourself get demoted.

If a lot of time has passed and no one has chosen to buy your property you need to ask yourself what you are doing wrong. Had you hired a realtor? Had you made sure that the house was clean? Had you renovated the kitchen and bathrooms?

Real Estate

You need to ensure that you followed every tip on this list, and if you have you need to reevaluate your property. See if your property was overpriced, if you missed something in either the home or the neighborhood. Ask your prospective buyers why they are not buying your property.

More often than not, your property is not being sold simply because the market is down, and if you wait you will find that buyers will come in and be interested even if you are doing everything the same way you did it before!

Chapter 7: Common Mistakes You Might Make

You know how to buy, you know how to sell, but you still might end up making these common mistakes. Don't be disheartened if you are committing one of the mistakes mentioned in this chapter. They are called common mistakes for a reason!

There are so many mistakes that are common to the way people conduct business in the real estate industry that this chapter is even longer than the previous chapter! Here is a list of mistakes you might be making:

Getting Tricked by the Decor/Not Remember the Sales Tips

Remember the aforementioned tip that involved setting your house up and decorating it so that your potential buyers like it more? You can fall for that trick too. If you enter a house that has been well decorated you might just miss all of the tiny little imperfections that the house might contain, and these imperfections would end up costing you dearly in the long run.

The seller that you are buying from is going to be using the same tricks that you are going to be using later on, and since you are buying for business you need to be even more alert than the average buyer. This means really getting into the core of the house and asking all of the right questions just to keep yourself safe from future problems.

This mistake can be easily avoided by hiring a home inspector. This is because home inspectors do not fall for such antics, they tend to get into the heart of the matter rather quickly and are not fooled by fancy furniture. Tricks that sellers use to hide defects in the property do not fool home inspectors, which is what makes them such a great investment for you.

Remember all of the tips that you were told in the buying chapter. Apply all of those tips to this transaction as well. Keep in mind that the seller is just as eager to sell this property off as you will be, so the exact same tricks apply.

Try to think of all of the tips you were provided on how to sell a house and try to compare these with what the seller is doing to his own property. This might help you to look past the decorations and see the true property.

Making it Difficult to Access Your House

One of the most common mistakes that people commit while they have their house open for viewing is not providing adequate parking to potential buyers. Not finding parking might make the buyers end up going to a different property. After all, they just don't know what you have to offer.

Not offering parking is also highly unprofessional. It gives the buyers a bad impression. After all, if you were thinking of buying a house wouldn't you be put off by the fact that you could not find parking anywhere near it?

The best thing you can do is to keep your driveway clear, and park your car on the street in front of your home. This way if anyone comes up to see your home you can move your car so that they can park there. This will facilitate two cars being parked in front of your house at once!

Additionally, you can have a friend or the realtor park their car in a different spot, securing it for any extra viewers you might get. Make it as easy for viewers and potential buyers to purchase your home as possible!

Not Attending any Community Meetings before Buying a Place

When your purchase your property, you are essentially buying the neighbors as well. If you want your house to have good property value you need to make sure that the property exists in an area with good people living in it.

You can be sure that any potential buyer worth his or her salt is going to check out the neighbors as well, just as much as you would end up checking out the neighborhood before buying a place yourself.

The best way to ensure that you are buying a house that is in a good neighborhood is to attend community meetings. A lot of different people attend community meetings, and attending them yourself is a good way to ensure that you are buying property in an area full of good people.

You can also find out a lot about the problems that people in the neighborhood face by attending these meetings. This is because most of the most troublesome aspects of the neighborhood are discussed in meetings such as this, which means that you can discover a lot that you would have to tackle before you buy your property or before you sell it.

Treating the Buying Process like an Auction

This is a very common mistake that people tend to make. The initial bid is an integral part of the whole process of buying a house, and should be made very carefully and after a lot of serious consideration. However, another important aspect is the final buying price.

This may seem obvious; after all you are buying the house for this amount. However, a lot of people tend to forget that there needs to be a clear line that you are not intending to cross while you are looking for properties to buy.

A lot of real estate professionals approach the purchasing of a property similarly to how they would approach an auction. This means that they keep outbidding people because they are dead set on buying the house.

This may seem like a good idea, but you might end up spending a lot more money than you can afford if you are not careful while bidding for your house.

In order to avoid a bidding war that you cannot afford, set a clear price in your head that you will not cross under any circumstances and stick to it at any cost.

Being a Salesman

You are selling your house, yes, but this does not make you a salesman. A salesman is widely considered to be a low creature, someone who is annoying and persistent, and who wants to take more than they are willing to give in return.

You need to be the kind of person that is giving the potential buyers a great gift, and you simply cannot do this by playing the salesman and making the hard sell while your potential buyers are viewing your house.

By doing this you are going to make potential buyers uncomfortable. Whatever you think is great about the house, you might not be able to express yourself properly to the buyer, or the buyer might just not feel the same way you do.

Doing this is also going to prevent your potential buyers from talking honestly and openly about what they do and do not like about the house. If they are not given an environment where they can express an honest opinion about a property that they are thinking of buying, they might not be comfortable enough to approach you or even the agent again no matter how much they like the property itself.

Waiting for the Right Time to Sell

You might remember from a couple of chapters ago that there is not particular way that you can measure when to sell your house. It's all about instinct and your own hard work at making the place look as good as possible.

One common and very serious mistake that a lot of people make is buying a house, renovating it and then sitting on it while waiting for the period of the year that is busiest as far as real estate goes: spring.

People need houses to live in, and they are looking to buy pretty much throughout the year. If your house is ready to view, set up some viewings!

Additionally, if you really want to wait for spring to sell your house, time your purchase accordingly. This will end up driving up the price of your house, but that's the price you pay by wanting to sell during the busy period.

It is highly recommended that you don't wait at all. Too many people wait to sell or try to time their transactions and it absolutely never works. In fact, it might just end up making you lose money.

Treating Real Estate like Stocks

The stock market is an exciting game to play. It is fast, it is very difficult to predict but the possibility of predicting something makes it that much more lucrative. If you can predict how a stock will behave you can turn bearish trends into goldmines and make unimaginable amounts of money!

This situation is highly ideal, however. Stocks are a very risky game to play, and often people who play the stock market end up penniless rather than rich.

Real estate is nothing like stocks. If you treat property the same way as stocks you are not going to end up doing yourself any favors. The real estate market is cyclical, yet unpredictable. It is not nearly as volatile as the stock market, so planning for ups and downs is detrimental in the long run.

A lot of people claim that real estate is not as big of a moneymaker as stocks. What they don't realize is that in real estate you just have to work hard and wealth is guaranteed. It is not a gamble in any way, and so is a lot more reliable than the stock market. Hence, you should not treat it the way you would stocks.

A Lack of Marketing

When you buy a home to sell, you really need to get into the marketing side of things. A lot of people don't realize that a concentrated effort needs to be made if you want to sell a home; it is a full time job that will take up a lot of your time.

Apart from renovating the house itself, you are going to have to spend a great deal of time actually marketing your home to people that would be interested in buying it.

A lot of people simply just put up a "For Sale" sign and believe that they can dust off their hands and congratulate themselves on a job well done. This is not the case.

You are going to have to approach a real estate agency and have them market your house in various different ways. These agencies have a client base and they can use this client base to make selling your house a lot easier for you.

You should also market your house using ads on social media websites. These ads are cheap and can reach a vast number of people that might be interested in buying your place.

Not Renovating to Sell

A lot of people tend to have the misconception that renovating your home is simple. It is not. If you are intending to sell your property off after renovating it you can't simply allow your renovations to be based on your own personal preferences, essentially what you would want in a house.

Instead, you need to appeal to the market. You need to understand what it is that buyers want so that you can give it to them. Renovating for yourself is pointless because your renovations will not appeal to as broad a group of people as possible.

If you really want to sell your home for a great price, as an interior decorator what kind of renovation would look good? Renovation is about design and style just as much as it is about making your house as good as new. This means that if you hire an interior designer, you can be rest assured that your buyers are going to be greatly impressed by the way your house looks.

If the interior designer is expensive, just consider it as an investment in the success of your home, a way to make it easier for you to sell and earn an income from real estate.

Depending on Virtual Tours

This is a rather amateurish mistake but if you are an amateur it is absolutely no reason to be ashamed. After all, you are still learning the ropes to this business and it's going to take time before you are fully equipped with the knowledge necessary to buy and sell real estate successfully.

If you find a property you like on the internet, you might be offered a virtual tour of the place. This is a great way to get a feel of the general layout of the house, along with any potential and resale value that it might have

However, it is important that you go and see the house yourself as well. Being physically present there is a lot different than being there through a virtual tour. These virtual tours usually only show the side of the house that the seller wants you to see after all.

As a result, you might end up missing a lot of problems that would affect the resale value. Approach this purchase like a professional and go see the house you are going to buy yourself.

Believing Real Estate Advertisements

As human beings, all of us tend to prefer the shorter route to everything. You might end up trying to take the shorter route while buying a house as well, and one of the biggest ways you can do this is caused by advertisements.

For example, if you see an ad that advertises a good neighborhood, you might subconsciously end up believing it. As a result you might not check the neighborhood out as thoroughly as you would have if you had not read such a comment on the advertisement.

One way in which you can tackle this problem is by reading advertisements and being doubly skeptical of the things that are advertised in the ad. Does it advertise a great neighborhood? View that with suspicion and keep a closer eye on the neighborhood. Travel there twice as much, engage in more community meetings.

By doing this you are going to ensure that you have all of your bases covered. You need to be sure that you know what you are doing when you buy a house to sell it, and it is important that you do not get beguiled by an ad, even if it happens at a subconscious level.

Choosing an Ineffectual Agent

Real Estate

Your realtor is your employee. This person is going to be one of the biggest factors in a business deal that is going to end up earning you a great deal of money. Hence, if you want to make sure that your house is sold without any mistakes or catastrophes, you need to make sure that the realtor you hire knows what he or she is doing.

A common mistake that people make is hiring realtors without really looking into them. You need to check the success rate of the realtor you hire, and ask around to see if they comport themselves with professionalism or not.

When you first meet the realtor you need to treat it like a job interview. After all, this person is going to be earning based on what you earn, so you need to be very careful in this aspect.

After a background check and interview, take a step back and think about whether the realtor is right for you or not. Getting the right realtor could mean that you set up a professional relationship that can help you in the long run as you can hire this realtor for every sale.

Not Hiring a Lawyer

Apart from the agent, you already know that there are a slew of other individuals who you are going to have to hire if you want the whole process of selling the house to be as efficient and stress free as possible.

A lot of these individuals are rather obvious, such as the renovators and the home inspector, along with the cleaning service. However, there is one individual that you might never have even thought of hiring, but you really should do so if you want the sale itself to go smoothly.

This individual is a lawyer. The contract that you are going to sign while transferring the ownership of the property to the buyer is a complex one, and must be looked over by someone who c an represent you legally.

Your lawyer should also look over a contract that you are going to sing while buying a property. There a lot of things that can go wrong here, and if you just take the effort, spend the money and hire a lawyer you are going to be able to save yourself a world of grief in the long run.

Buying Expensive Property

As a businessman you might think that buying expensive property is the smart thing to do. After all, you buy an expensive commodity you are going to get a similarly high return when you finally sell the commodity off right?

If you read the previous chapters you will know that the most expensive property is not the most profitable. Expensive properties don't appreciate that much, and can end up selling for too little profit to have been worth the effort of scouting, buying, remodeling and all of the extra expenses such as property tax, home inspectors, lawyers etc. You might end up not making money at all.

Avoid this mistake and buy cheaper property. If you buy a decent place in a neighborhood that is about average you can get it for cheap and make it so that it sells for a lot higher than you bought it for. Cheaper places have much more room to appreciate than more expensive places.

Think of it as a price cap. After a certain price, you are going to start alienating potential buyers. In order to avoid this, do the smart thing and invest in fixer uppers or cheaper properties.

Setting an Unrealistic Budget

This is also a very common problem. A lot of us don't buy properties with our own money, we use a mortgage to pay for it and pay the bank off with monthly installments. Until the mortgage is paid off, the bank is the actual owner of the car.

The mistake that is made regards the size of the loan that we take. You might be cleared for a rather large loan, one that could even consist of several hundred thousand dollars. You might have access to tens of thousands, maybe even a hundred or two, more than you need to buy a good property and then sell it.

This can cause problems in the long run. If you have bought a property, you are going to have to pay it off too. Before you take the loan ask yourself, are you going to be able to make every monthly payment? What if you can't sell the house fast enough?

You need to take everything into account while you are taking your loan from the bank. If you are haphazard and set an unrealistic budget, you might end up missing payments and would lose the house as a result.

Not Visiting the House Several Times

You already know that you have to visit the house instead of relying on a virtual tour and you have probably already done this. However, the mistake you might be making is just visiting it that one time and not doing so again until you actually buy it.

Even if the first time you visited the property you did so with a home inspector, you are probably going to have to visit several times more if you want to make sure that the property doesn't have anything that you might be missing.

After all, the seller probably knew that you were going to bring a home inspector and might have arranged the house in such a way that certain areas became inaccessible or blocked from view.

Hence, you should visit the house three or four times before you buy it. Visit once with a home inspector, once with your partner, once with a friend, and one time just visit all on your own and get a feel for the place.

This is going to be the thing earning you money. Being thorough is not just recommended, it's necessary.

Being Lazy While Closing

Do not, under any circumstances, leave everything for the last minute while closing a deal. Whether you are closing a purchase or a sale, treat it like a job and get everything done ahead of time so that there is no reason to be worried when the big day arrives.

There are a lot of documents that you can get well before the actual closing day. You can have your lawyer draw up the paperwork well before you have to close the deal. Alternatively, you can have your own lawyer go through the contract as many times as you want him or her to. This will help ensure that no loopholes are missed and that the deal goes down smoothly.

A lot of paperwork can be received around twenty four hours before the deal has to be made. You should get it as soon as it is available. Waiting for the last moment will only make it that much more likely that something goes wrong. Believe me when I tell you that things going wrong at the last minute involve one of the most severe kinds of stress that you can think of and is well worth avoiding.

One of the most important things that you can do while closing is getting the home inspector to do one last check of the home before you buy it. Anything he catches at this moment is going to be something that you will not have to worry about later, and is very important in the long run.

You can also run through the house you are about to sell yourself. Find anything that the buyer might not like and make sure that everything is spick and span. While the contract is being signed make sure that you have your lawyer present and just be as proactive as possible during the whole process.

Going too big With the Renovations

When we say renovations, we are talking about minor renovations that are not that expensive to get done. A common mistake that a lot of people make is that they end up remodeling the entire house.

This is essential as far as fixer uppers are concerned, but most of the time large scale renovation work is simply not worth the hassle. It turns into a full on construction job that will end up costing way more than you expected.

Large scale renovations usually take up a considerable amount of time for completion. This is because construction workers and renovators tend to stretch out projects in order to get paid more.

As a result, your home will end up costing way too much to be profitable. If you want to renovate, and you should, do minor remodeling projects. Fix up the bath tub, get a new commode, but don't do anything that will completely change the face of the house that you are about to sell because it is simply too risky a task to undertake.

What you really need to renovate is your front lawn. Curb appeal, as you already know from the previous chapter, is one of the biggest factors in your sale because it is what actually invites people into your home.

If you are spending big money, spend it on your front lawn and front porch. Make it seem as attractive as possible. This is a great investment because there is only so much that can be done if you remain tasteful, and it has an actual measurable effect on the efficiency with which your home will end up getting sold.

Not Getting Pre Approved

You already know that getting pre approved is a big part of the whole process of buying a home. A lot of people tend not to realize this and instead go for the process that is simpler by becoming pre qualified. Some people even skip the prequalification part and just head into the house hunting process!

If you get pre approved for your mortgage you are going to be showing your potential seller that you really want to buy a house. You are showing seriousness and that is an important part of the whole process.

Buying Property after Little Haggling

Haggling is a very important part of the entire process of buying or selling a place. Within the context of buying, however, it becomes particularly significant.

A lot of people don't haggle enough before buying something. They might think that the price is fair, or that they cannot get a better place within a comparable price range. As a result, they decide to take the place. This also stems from laziness, as some people just can't be bothered to check other places out before deciding to buy, thinking that the difference in price is too little to care about.

You need to check out other places in the neighborhood to find a decent price. Additionally, if you haggle for a lower price and get a deal, you should be suspicious of it.

This is because most sellers are unwilling to lower the price because they will have spent a great deal of money getting the place ready for sale. Hence, you should expect a great deal of haggling to occur, and you probably won't get a price that is as low as your first offer because the seller might end up losing money this way.

Hence, if a seller is willing to agree to your first bid without any kind of fuss that is a good reason to be suspicious. If he or she is so eager to sell at such a low price there is a good chance that something is wrong with the place.

This doesn't mean that you have to run. The seller might have realized that the price was too high, or they are just desperate to sell and aren't smart enough to not let it show. However, this is cause for alertness. Proceed with caution in such situations.

Going for the First Property You Check Out

It happens, and is just a part of human nature. When you really get into the process of buying real estate in order to sell it you are going to be excited, and that excitement is probably going to taint your judgment and make you end up buying the first property that you check out.

You might even end up fighting a house that is absolutely perfect in every way. It has no major problems, will require minimal renovation and is even within your price range, making it something that you absolutely have to buy!

However, one piece of advice that you absolutely must adhere to is that nobody should ever buy the first property they see. No matter how good it looks, something is going to be wrong with it, or there is going to be a property out there that is a lot better.

When you check out a house it is very important that you check out other houses in the area as well. Try to check out three or four more and ask for the prices. This will give you a price range that will give you an idea of whether the house was overpriced or not.

Even if it was perfect, the seller might have seen your enthusiasm and would have bulked up the price a little hoping to take advantage of it. You might even find a better house for the same price or less, you might discover that someone got murdered in that house which is why it's so cheap.

The best thing to do is to gather as much data as possible and to evaluate what you have found after collecting everything. This will allow you to make an informed decision which is going to help you in the long run.

Not Getting a Good Inspector

When you buy a home you are going to have it inspected before you sign the contract. With the emphasis that has been placed on how important that is you are probably going to, otherwise you will not be doing what this book is telling you to do.

However, a major mistake that a lot of people make is that they do not hire good inspectors. By good, we mean expensive, because the more expensive an inspector is the more thorough of a job he is going to do while checking your potential property out for defects.

Obviously, inspectors can be overpriced too. However, it is still extremely important that you go for inspectors that are in the higher price ranges so that you can be sure that you are getting someone who you can force to check as much as you want him or her to.

You can also ask for a lot of extra material such as written reports and photographs that you might not be able to with a lower paid inspector, as they tend to be lazier since they are not getting paid enough.

Real Estate

Buying For Yourself Rather Than the Market

As a real estate professional, it is very important that you look at the homes you are buying as commodities that you are going to sell. You are not going to live in these homes, you are going to make them look good and sell them for however much you can.

Hence, your feelings on what the house is like are irrelevant. If you do not like the house but know that the average buyer will absolutely love it, you don't have to worry about your own feelings on the matter.

Your tastes and the tastes of the average buyer might not align. You might not like a certain neighborhood because it will feel too pretentious but a buyer might come in and absolutely love it. After all, some people like to live in high class neighborhoods. These people will pay you good money to provide for them a home in such a neighborhood!

You might be into a neighborhood with culture, but some people might not be interested in that sort of thing. Hence, buying a property in this neighborhood is simply not going to be profitable for you in any real way. Instead it is just going to be a burden that you will have to bear and will probably end up losing you money.

There should be a checklist of things that each house you are buying should have. Once you have formed a professional relationship with a realtor you can ask him or her about what would be a good list of things that a home you are looking to sell should have.

This way you can find homes that at least have the capacity to include such features, even if they do not include such features in the first place.

Pricing Your Property Incorrectly

A lot of people are surprised at how much work goes into a real estate. A lot of this work is actually research, as almost half of the work involved in real estate requires you to conduct rigorous, thorough research that will take a long time to complete.

Real Estate

One area of the entire business transaction that requires perhaps the most significant amount of research is the selling price. Your selling price is a very important part of your transaction, because a lot of people tend to price their houses too high due to a lack of knowledge regarding the market prices.

An important part of conducting research is to look up similar homes in the neighborhood. Ask people who live near the property you own what they think of the price you are setting, and whether it is comparable to the price that they paid for their own home. You can adjust for inflation and changes in property price based on how long ago they made the purchase and gauge the price of your own home accordingly.

If you fail to do so, the repercussions could be rather inconvenient, especially if you were planning on selling your home quickly. If your price is too high, buyers might reject the place outright.

You might have to eventually lower the price, and this is never a good sign. If you are reducing the price, buyers might end up thinking that there is some sort of defect in the place, and that you are lowering your price to cover it up.

Lowering your price once might also make buyers think that you are desperate for a sale, which would make them aggressive in their bargaining tactics. It will make it difficult for you to sell your house for a competitive price at all.

Chapter 8: Commercial Real Estate Tips

The world of commercial real estate is completely different from residential real estate. The way you approach the situation is going to be altered, and you will have to be wary of different things.

This warranted a separate chapter for commercial real estate. Hence, in this chapter you are going to be provided with a series of tips that will tell you how to approach the buying and selling of commercial real estate for profit. It is a very profitable enterprise as long as you get these basic rules, tricks and tips down!

Get Certified

Dealing in commercial real estate is actually very different from dealing in residential real estate. One of the biggest differences is that you have to get certified in order to properly deal with commercial property.

By becoming a Certified Commercial Investment member you are not just going to get access to contacts that will help you sell commercial real estate. Additionally, it will be a bit like a pre approved loan in that it will show potential sellers that you are serious about your desire to purchase commercial property and will treat the transaction with the utmost respect.

Go For Expensive Property

Yes, in this aspect the world of commercial real estate might just be the complete opposite of residential real estate. Whereas in residential real estate you are expected to by cheap because expensive properties do not appreciate as much, commercial properties demand a different approach.

With commercial real estate it pays to go big if you can afford it. This is because commercial real estate is always hot, and expensive places are always being searched for, particularly in this day and age where startups are being created almost every day. These startups need office space, and you will be the one to provide it.

Find Someone to Help You

The world of commercial real estate is rather difficult to traverse on your own. You are unable to get a grasp of things quickly enough to get anything done in the initial stages.

Hence, it is very useful to have a mentor in these initial stages. A mentor can really help you by showing the ropes and giving you tips and tricks that you might not have thought of one your own. The mentor can also help you to get contacts within the real estate industry.

Don't Rush

This applies to both buying as well as selling. If you find a good property, take your sweet time dealing with it. Look at as many properties in as many locations as you possibly can.

This is one of the most important parts of real estate in the commercial sector. If research comprises the majority of what residential real estate is about then it is ninety nine percent of what commercial real estate is about. There really is little more than you can use in real estate than the ability to research and gather data, and analyze said data in an effective manner.

In fact, commercial real estate takes a really long time to get into. This is especially true for cash flow. Even if you just jump right into it, you are going to have to take your time before selling because it just doesn't happen that quickly with commercial real estate.

The first few months of your journey as a commercial real estate businessman are going to have to be spent checking out as much real estate as possible, even real estate that is not suitable for you to buy. This will allow you to form a price range in your head and find out what areas are the most expensive.

You are also going to find out through this technique the various factors that go into the price of a commercial property. This is very important because since commercial properties are so highly valuable, buying and selling them involves a lot more corner cutting and cunning on the part of the people you are dealing with.

In order to be able to deal with this you will need as much information as you can get about the commodities you are investing in. By taking your time and doing your research you are going to become an expert at commercial real estate, and will be able to monetize your knowledge very quickly as a result.

Keep Investing in Residential Property on the Side

One major fact that you need to understand about commercial real estate is that it is never an entry level game. Commercial real estate is more of a level up that you should only undertake if you have significant financial security, because you are not going to be earning a lot of money any time soon if doing this right is your top priority.

Hence, it is important that you keep investing in residential properties on the side. This will allow you to maintain your cash flow and ensure that you have enough funds to support you while you are doing research on your commercial properties.

You will obviously also need cash to get into the commercial real estate business once you have gathered enough information to do it right. Possessing liquid assets is important because you might need to pay anything at any time and having liquid assets such as cash will allow you to pay for these things without harming your credit rating or boosting your debt.

Apart from financial security and investment capital, it is important to start with residential properties because that is the best way to gain experience. Residential real estate is a far more docile enterprise than commercial real estate because there is a much more supportive and accommodating environment involved.

Getting involved in residential real estate before moving on to commercial real estate allows you to learn how real estate works. It allows you to learn how to deal with potential buyers, how to vet and treat you real estate agents, what you'll need to do to ensure that property is worth buying.

It will also show you how to handle contracts and money. Both of these things can get incredibly tricky when commercial plots get involved. This is because commercial property gets involved in business, and all business involves some kind of compromise. You will have to make sure that you are not the one that has to end up compromising in this situation.

All in all, commercial property is incredibly lucrative but at the same time is quite risky too. It's better to get a hang of real estate in general by investing in residential properties than by

Getting Your Property Appraised is Difficult

There is subjectivity involved in practically every area of the world of real estate. If you are experienced in the realm of residential real estate you will be familiar that getting a value for your property is a fairly annoying procedure.

However, in the world of commercial real estate the process isn't annoying, it's downright frustrating. This is because a lot more subjectivity is involved, the ambience of a place can be more of a factor. Surprisingly, people tend to care more about where they are planning to work rather than where they are planning to live!

Thus, it is important that you get acquainted with the entire valuation process for commercial real estate. This can be done by asking your mentor, or if you have not gotten a mentor yet you can purchase a commercial property for a practice run.

If you do this prepare for a long hard slog while selling it and don't expect to earn a lot of money. You simply won't have the experience at this point to be able to traverse the hostile landscape of commercial property, as this is just a learning experience for you.

Location Beats Property

Real Estate

When you buy a property in a residential area, the location plays an important role. The neighborhood that the house resides in can dictate the price in a lot of ways. However, at the end of the day, the major role is played by the house itself.

If the house is excellent, it will be bought at a good price even if it's in a neighborhood that is not that great. There is a small margin, and ratio that you can use to ascertain whether the neighborhood is good enough that the quality of the house can take care of the rest.

However, with commercial real estate location is everything. Money will be riding on how good the location is. If you buy a fantastic office building in a remote location you aren't going to get any buyers.

This is because your building will involve a lot of extra expenditures for the company or entity that purchases it. They will have to install a cafeteria because there will be no restaurants nearby, a dreary location would result in low productivity, and people would have a long commute that they would have to get through in order to get to work.

This is why location is extremely important. A great location can help to sell off the property as quickly as possible. People will be able to commute to it more easily, they will have plenty of places to eat, and the area will always be bustling with activity facilitating a positive work environment.

Hence, if it is a tossup between property and location, always go for location. Great property means nothing in the world of commercial real estate, which is one of the biggest reasons why this world is so different from the world of residential real estate.

Partner Up

This might be an odd concept to you. However, the more risk you face the more partners you should have. This is one of the biggest reasons why public companies exist, because all of the shareholders are partners.

This is mostly so that debt can be distributed, which essentially means that no single person is liable if an enterprise fails. This is not really necessary in residential real estate unless you are short on investment capital. Otherwise, residential real estate is an extremely safe endeavor.

In commercial real estate, however, a lot more risk is involved. This risk often involves investment capital as well, which tends to be much, much higher where commercial properties are concerned. It is also important to have someone that can help shoulder the debt if the property does not sell for a long period of time.

Apart from all of these reasons, sometimes it is necessary just to have someone who is just as invested in this enterprise as you are. You can talk to this person seriously and objectively about the problems you are facing without letting emotions get in the middle of it.

Having such a thing is truly helpful, especially in an enterprise such as investment in commercial real estate, so do yourself a favor and get yourself a partner!

Vet Your Partner

Getting a partner is important, but it is equally important to make sure that this partner is trustworthy. If your answer is yes, you are wrong.

As far as money is concerned, absolutely no one is trustworthy until you have done a complete background check and vetted them until you have little reasonable doubt. Even in such situations, reasonable doubt remains, thus creating a lack of trust between you and your partner.

This is not an entirely bad thing. So much money is involved that a little bit of mistrust can actually be healthy. It can help bring a modicum of honesty to your business dealings, which is a very important part of the whole process, particularly in an industry where dishonesty has become so rampant.

One major tip that you must follow is to never go in business with people you are friends with. This is especially true for people you love, such as your wife or a relative.

Real Estate

This is because when you go into business with such people, you tend to look at everything through a lens. This lens prevents you from seeing what is truly in front of you.

As a result, your friend might be stealing your money but you would never know because you trust him so much. This would really hurt your enterprise in the long run.

Hence, always stay on the safe side. Don't ever make someone you are friends with or related to a partner, and whoever you do make your partner make sure that they are trustworthy. After all, this is how you earn your living and bring food to the table.

Conclusion

I thank you once again for choosing this book and hope you had a good time reading it.

As is apparent, each type of property has its own pros and cons. choosing the type will depend on how much profit you wish to make from your investment.

The next step is for you to choose a type of property to invest your money in.

Although all three make for great options, you can choose to go with commercial properties if you are a beginner and then move to the other types after you gain confidence to deal in properties. But whatever that you choose, you must pay attention to the various details of the property as mentioned in chapter 1 and make your choice once you are satisfied with it.

I hope you make the right choice for yourself and reap the fruits of your labor at the earliest.

Good luck!

www.ingramcontent.com/pod-product-compliance
Lightning Source LLC
Chambersburg PA
CBHW070940180526
45168CB00003B/1115